Painstaker

Painstaker

Poems

Jeffrey Galbraith

RESOURCE *Publications* • Eugene, Oregon

PAINSTAKER
Poems

Copyright © 2017 Jeffrey Galbraith. All rights reserved. Except for brief quotations in critical publications or reviews, no part of this book may be reproduced in any manner without prior written permission from the publisher. Write: Permissions, Wipf and Stock Publishers, 199 W. 8th Ave., Suite 3, Eugene, OR 97401.

Resource Publications
An Imprint of Wipf and Stock Publishers
199 W. 8th Ave., Suite 3
Eugene, OR 97401

www.wipfandstock.com

PAPERBACK ISBN: 978-1-5326-1821-5
HARDCOVER ISBN: 978-1-4982-4359-9
EBOOK ISBN: 978-1-4982-4358-2

Manufactured in the U.S.A.

For Paula, love's best tutor

Contents

I.

God the Gorilla or Wolf | 3
The Garbage Fires | 4
Bloodlines | 5
Fields a Green Wave | 6
Who Do You Say I Am | 7
Record of Persons Whose Names Have Changed | 9
With My Father, Cutting Pigs | 10
When Matt's Dad Lost His Hand | 11
Menagerie Wish List | 12
Frankenthumb | 13
Captain of the Wrestling Team and His Best Friend, During Practice | 15
Our Last High School Summer | 16
Metamorphosis | 17
In the Kitchen | 18
Come Spring | 19
Cloud Sheep | 21

II.

How We Got a Dog | 25
Lobster through the Heavens | 26
At the Pacific | 28
Day of the Dead, *Michoacán* | 29
First Date, Valentine's Day | 30
Letter from the Corner of Lemons and Main | 32

Wish List in Middle Age | 34
My Resurrected Body | 35
Painstaker | 36
Love Wins | 37
Elegy for Deer-Man | 39
Unbidden | 40
Hope New Rising | 41
re Controversy | 42
Poem with Italicized Phrases from a Student's Water-Stained Mythology Class Notes, Found Perched on a Vanishing Bank of Snow | 44

III.

Sonnet | 47
Isaiah in the Cancer Ward | 48
Down in the Head | 49
Isaiah in Chicagoland | 51
Shop-soiled, *adj.* | 52
The Poet Abuzz after Chemo on a Whammo Steroid | 53
Early Christian Advice Column | 54
New Life, Lake Scituate | 55
Prayer | 56
Elevation, St. Louis Arch | 57
Elegy for a Poet Catching Stride | 58
I Dream Your Face the Night You Move Away | 61
Winter Monarchs, *Michoacán* | 62
Killdeer | 63
Self-Portrait as Motel Night Clerk | 64
Two Decades Gone, *Barra de Navidad* | 70
Isaiah on the Promise of International Space Projects | 71

Acknowledgements

"Concerning International Space Projects" and "Phrases from a Student's Water-Stained Index Card," published in *Florida Review*

"Early Christian Advice Column," published in *Windhover*

"Fields a Green Wave," published in *RHINO*

"New Life, Lake Scituate" and "Day of the Dead, *Michoacan*," published in *Cresset*

"Prayer," published in *Sensucht*

"Record of Persons Whose Names Have Changed," published in *Southern Humanities Review*

"When Matt's Dad Lost His Hand," published in *Yemassee*

I.

God the Gorilla or Wolf

God the gorilla or wolf
Who cannot be named
Who sits preening me, cracking

lice, upping the shine
Who knocks me over
with His teeth

and expressionless lips
Who noses the soft parts underneath
Who rages at my bellygods

at my other beloveds
Who sets out His own feast
Who row by row across

the unearthly white
of the scalp scrapes up
what He can eat

Who numbers my hands, my eyes
Who has motherhen guile
Who cannot be distant only

Who will not play by my rules

The Garbage Fires

Flames darken cans of tin,
half burn the labels, pop
gristle off the chicken bones.
I watch a milk jug melt

into a twisting face.
The city won't come out
this far. We farm beyond
the line where garbage trucks

turn back, so we dug a hole
behind the house to burn
the trash, or maybe the dark
sat gaping there before

we came. Who knows who first
crouched over a fresh-dug
pit to hide his shame. When
my father burned his porn,

I wasn't meant to see
the photos only half-burned,
like young, green saplings on
the smoking pyre. My snooping

is what put them there
and how I knew to rescue them.
Next day, I carried myself
full of secret life to school.

Bloodlines

My son with the Spanish name is exactly like me. It's striking how handsome and smart he is. How winsome. As if we came from the same parents. As if he were not a diluted version of me. I almost wish I had refused to circumcise him, just so people could tell us apart.

It's striking how my wife loves each of us practically the same. How she grafted him to her breast. The way she cradles and frets over him. She would do anything for us. Even chew off her own arm if it was caught in a trap and a cheetah slunk through the tall grass to where her husband-baby lay on a blanket enjoying the afternoon. Even if the predator were a spider,

which she usually runs from screaming. I swear she would turn around, risk it all to come back for us. That's the difference family makes. And why I have no fear of growing old. Of waking one day unable to recognize my own face.

Fields a Green Wave

Almost as thick as the young corn
on our farm were the flies, breeding

on more and more manure
from the hogs. You kept your mouth

closed walking around. Reach
your hand into the buzzing fog

and you'd catch clod after clod.
Once I caught two stuck tight,

a shudder in air, stone-faced, just
as they began to soar a great distance.

Lost to myself I think on them,
how the rich dung intrudes

into nearby towns,
where the thick smells waft, come down.

Who Do You Say I Am

To the pissed-off colleague
I look like the cat that ate the canary,
whereas the panhandler

outside Home Depot says
I look like Drew Carey,
so I ask him for my dollar back.

The same week a drive-thru
worker swears I look exactly
like that guy who plays for the Packers,

and I remember how years ago,
an older, hairier teen cornered me
after football practice to say

You know, you're one ugly motherfucker.
But who can really say? At the airport,
the lead vocalist for an R&B group

mistook me for the singer
of another R&B group and O
how I wanted to take her backstage.

Even the cloudless sky is blue
with longing. I remember
one time a neighbor-farmer

thought out loud I might be *funny*,
so dad put me to work
with the hogs and I watched

WHO DO YOU SAY I AM

from the trees as he called for me
through outbuildings and barn,
his anger on my name.

Built anxious, I feared legion
in the swine, spooked at the sound
of shades on the stair,

had not yet learned to thrill
in becoming stranger, more
distant from myself.

Record of Persons Whose Names Have Changed

> From an exhibit of eighteenth-century documents at the public
> library, Chelmsford, Mass.

All is vanity. The man who changed Bumside

to Burnside, afraid of himself, the protuberance of it,
hanging there for whoever

might use it to demean him or make dirty. In such cases,
the rubbed-out letters

shelter and shield, Lorenzo
rechristened Larry, in the daybreak

of state function:
Be it enacted, &c., as follows . . .

The magic is immediate. The new name a sandpaper
smoothing away bumps

and unsightly knobs—a flatline of your former self.
For others, before and after pictures

show no perceptible change, no clearing away of trees

or rocks from the rich, black soil. As in the case
of Micajah, who strangely

insisted on Morrill. What neighbor haunted him?
What hope of safety? What millstone

kept him just out of reach of the surface, that intoxication
of air that comes

from standing aloof, unknown, amid the rabble?

With My Father, Cutting Pigs

Finally I learn to hold, raise
the small one

head-down, hock-spread,
        to stretch flat the skin,

my hands raw around
        the bristled hooves.

Bending low, my father
makes two quick cuts, kneads

the skin to surface them.
        With enough practice I turn

the pig quick so my father
can scissor the tail.

As the squealing fades
into a burst of grunts,

        I hold out to him the next.

When Matt's Dad Lost His Hand

We comforted Matt on the school bus—*Does he have a fake one now?*
Then somebody made fun of Bunny Lip, aka Leon

Stinks, aka Stutter Step, and he boxed wild as the bus
turned from blacktop roads to gravel, past scraping

harvesters, the eaten fields, dropping us off one by one. We trudged
the lane to the house, heads bowed looking for rocks

to throw at sparrows on the fence line. Everything tensed
    when we appeared, angered by hunger, lowing with milk.

Menagerie Wish List

If I could, I would buy an exotic live animal for every room of the house. Two lion cubs in the bedroom as the emblem of innocent risk-taking. A giraffe in the foyer drawing the eye upward to our gorgeous cathedral ceilings. Maybe a gorilla with thumbs to help in the kitchen. In the bathroom, with its tropical steam and rot, a parrot for my feathered mirror. If we had an attached garage, I could go for a monkey—one of those cotton-top tamarins we saw at the Museum of Science (they looked like little old men, gymnastic and wise). For the kids' rooms who knows, since they are animals still. The small one continues to take food from my hand, and none of them is entirely self-grooming. Though I keep purchasing their food, already it's plain I won't be their master for long.

Frankenthumb

Let the mind spin with the baby-faced
farm kid who grabbed

the spell-casting
spinning of the tractor as it drilled

the PTO shaft powering the auger-belt
that floated the fresh-baled straw

to the top shelf of the barn loft.
Let the mind spin as the farm kid

grabbed the spinning shaft
and was thrown.

It happened quick as spin,
the rag-doll kid tossed clear

by the spinning shaft, thumb and finger
torn from him, gone up in smoke,

never to be heard from again.
Let it sink in how they fixed his grip

by severing his big right toe,
dropping the toe

into a tub of parts which they shook
and stirred and shook again

to make him new. Let it cycle
in the news

FRANKENTHUMB

that the toe now sits bolted on
where the thumb once was,

looking out of place but hey,
so would you, after thirteen years

laced-up, hooded inside the shoe.

Captain of the Wrestling Team and His Best Friend, During Practice

He'll admit he bit me.
Tangled up somehow I floated against

his teeth. I swore loud, slapped him
around some, held him so others could too.

Nobody really cared. Coach said
I wouldn't screw up that move ever again.

But what if I had only paused,
as when my finger brushed the hot stove,

the singe unsettling, myself
not unsettled?

My quiet then would have meant more
than an entire weekend

without calling, more than a cold shoulder
after all our double dates, swapped

clothes, six-packs. Together as the like-ends
of magnets we would have slipped

from each other in that silence, one
invisibly pushing

the other away. As it was, he jumped up,
tackling me to claim:

   I'll bite it clean off, Captain!
And we rested on each other like sons.

Our Last High School Summer

Our 4th of July is cherry bombs
popping around the cars lined up,

parked at lake's edge. We put
the top down for the best view,

blast Bad Company and then
Hendrix goes crazy

on the anthem as we dream out loud
of college girls and fish so many

they fight for the worm-fat hook.
At dark when the fireworks begin,

we're two six-packs in
and the man on the truck bed

next to us yells, in so many words,
that fire defends the flag

and those who torch the fabric
will be burned in turn.

We climb out of the car
to shoot bottle rockets from our fingers

like glorious birds set free,
defending our lakefront heaven.

Metamorphosis

    You head-fake and leap
into the end zone, wiry strong, star
of the field. Anything to dull being downsized,
running a store now. Enter the haughty
former co-worker—
                        your eyes stay on the floor
as you push the broom up close to those black
leather boots reaching up like hands
to her glorious knees.

    You are whittled down by wind, alone
in a blighted field. She is too swift for you
and nibbles at your hand, bolting away on her crisp

black hooves with a flip of white. It grows dark
and furious. You don't want to shoot her

anymore, heavy the bullets that are all these years.

In the Kitchen

Released, he cleaned food
from plates, crusted cheese and taco shells,
the spray nozzle taken up lightly

then swung to hit the fajita tin
or enchilada platter so water might splash
on a passing waitress, to get her attention.

One week out of prison he was energetic,
determined, skittish still. I showed him how to mix
a bucket of margaritas for the bar

and we sat back to taste our work.
Arson, he offered, before I could ask. *But that's not
the way it happened.* He got emotional then,

told me don't be a fuck-up and I should always
stay in school, as fruit flies drew to the sugared pail.

Come Spring

Come up for
the season maybe
find work

guiding the hardplow
talk sweet
to the backsides

of the draft horses
The man's wife
brings a pail

spigot on the bottom
and hangs it
full of water

on a tree limb after dark
though the shower
won't get you

hardly clean after
making rows all day
and the two kids

sneak from the house
to watch stove-hot
water runnel

through the dirt
I wear like wages
on my arms, my neck

COME SPRING

They don't know
me from Adam or dare
to know

sure as the horses
stretch to my
hand come spring

Cloud Sheep

The farmer settles into an overstuffed
chair, looks up at the crafts gilding
the shelf above the living room,
scrap wood cut with a jig saw into
clouds and adorned with Bible verses

and cotton balls to form religious sheep.
They enter his thoughts as he reclines,
closes the daily devotional left there
by his artistic, devoted wife. In his
dream, one of the sheep sparks a panic

by moving beyond the woolen herd.
The wooden animal sheers himself,
gives his coat to those colder than he,
and dons a sandwich board to warn,
Choose today whom you will serve!

Stripped down to a string of words,
he is no longer fluffy or comforting.
The stark verse taunts his shelf mates,
who hold themselves head down,
eye deep in delicious grass. As the news

spreads the sheep begin to swell
with tears. The lone one violates nature
and so the clouds begin to storm.
Darkened with dirt clods and bits of straw,
their gale force suddenly knocks him

CLOUD SHEEP

tumbling into the magazine caddy
under the flat-screen. Startled,
the man wakes to ads for phone sex
and miracle stain removers, blind hope
in various forms. The harvest done, soon

he'll drive truck for the winter months.
As he rises from the chair, he thinks maybe
he'll put the naked sheep on the dash
as a caution to savor coastal cities
and wide right turns, the far off sky,
                all these are his reward.

II.

How We Got a Dog

    After Ashbery's "Two Scenes"

Soft around the middle, answerable to none,
we refuse to pity the horde of homeless
former pets. Why should we? Our train arrives
with joy each day. Despite the wet grass of years,
we spark like dry tinder, sharpened
not dulled by the clashes of our needs.
Like it says in the Bible, the sun shines

on Sahara and glacier, simple as math.
But try telling that to the homeless animals
gathering outside our window. As the day
caresses us with sunlight, they arrive like spores
on the leftovers, foul-smelling, ribs almost nude,

a literal pestilence of pets, killing the grass.
They speak in unison, like a Chorus: *Hey, asshole*,
they say. *We can see you through the curtains*.
I look at my wife, who shrugs, plays the submissive.
You wear the pants, she says.

The train slides from the tracks onto the wet grass
of years toward a rare minor collision, mere glitch,
an opportunity really, this clatter of barking, this pull
of sacrifice to new altars.

Lobster through the Heavens

    After departing Boston Logan International Airport

Bottom crawler trapped in a box
in the overhead, your fate is compounded

at the hands of tourists recently seen
gaping in the New England Aquarium. I too

think you are tasty, have sucked
the meat of your claws, the hot sweat

of your butter. Now you jostle like a cat
in a carrier, delicious pet amid turbulence.

I once had a delicious pet: Alesha,
my bottle-fed calf, my wide-eyed girl,

became sumptuous steak. My parents gave
us both our daily bread, and one day

they served her instead. My sister,
the vegetarian, would soon convert,

but I am no less your friend
for being deaf to your pain.

Crustacean, your cross is light.
Soon you shall be a child's foretaste

of Boston, or perhaps a husband's
barter for the love of an in-law.

LOBSTER THROUGH THE HEAVENS

Never will you age or divorce or rage
unthinking at those closest

to your heart. Together let us dream
through the waters above,

raised as we are
from the bottomless dark of the whale-road.

At the Pacific

What I still picture about that weekend
is the silhouette theater of the fishermen.
On a cracked stage of rocks, they worked
a silent ocean audience. Like magicians

with quick wrists they plucked fish
from the blank face of the water,
and the fish clapped their bodies on the rocks
in the moonlight. With hook and string,

father taught child an age-old trade,
swiveling the hips to make the taut line sing.
As for you and me watching the stars

from the sand, what I still don't
understand is that glancing blow of your eyes
and the chill of your body later, as lifeless

to me as the catch the fishermen
collected before the rain clouds burst forth
and kissed them home with their winnings.

Day of the Dead, *Michoacán*

She takes me to a cemetery over roads
lined with stone walls that lilting flowers top
and spill over, bougainvilleas

battling the wind. We discuss hair
and its embellishments because she's
in beauty school and wants

to brush and color me.
I'd rather she loan me her clothes,
add red to my lips,

and I'll be plush and flit
around the moonlit, somber tombs.
Isn't this a holiday? Where are the pumpkins?

I'm bored with walking, so she pulls out
our snack: cookies shaped like skulls
with proper, frosted names—

the hairless, sugared heads of relatives.
I taste the icing of a crumbling
brow—*not bad*—of someone she says

I'll meet tonight. The person in my teeth
melts like a wafer, an accepted
invitation to the party later, to meet

the baldness of death, as the wind
draws us up to the cemetery
running its tongue around my head.

First Date, Valentine's Day

Perhaps it was the mid-line luxury car
you arrived in, leather seats and seat
warmers, that managed to take the edge off
the cold night, the pressure
of starting this date on a day littered
with the offal of sophomore love, the traumas
of plastic hearts, blood roses, and novelty

chocolate body parts. The Anti-Valentine's
Day party held by your friends was also
a relief, for reasons other than those of two
co-workers emerging rumpled, pleased,
from the bedroom. You and I were anticipation
and mystery, dizzy in a cloud of pent-up
unknowing. Or perhaps I should speak
only for myself, temperature rising
with each mouthful of chipotle bean dip.
But how else to explain our awkward, shared

silence at the liquor store earlier?
The task of bringing a six-pack had suddenly
seemed a test, a gust of questions billowing forth
from the open cooler door. Dark or light? Micro-
brew or major brand? Thick or thin? Better or worse?
Deciding to decide at random we walked
to the register, where I worked to disguise

my shock as the price rang up an amount
unheard of in the history of malt and hops.
A pall fell over the room. Time stopped.
The cashier looked directly into my eyes,
as if dropping a glove: Would I pony up
to impress the lady? Or would I retreat to the cooler,

FIRST DATE, VALENTINE'S DAY

beet red, for something cheaper? I ponied.
Imagine my relief back in the car, when
you said what I hoped you were thinking:
>*That must be miracle beer. Let's hide it*
>*at the party so no one else can have any.*
In the apartment full of people, our secret
worked like your breath on my neck. Your eyes
from across the room spoke an intimacy
of embarrassment overcome, a pact
that would serve us for the long haul,
a new-formed alliance of the unspoken.

Letter from the Corner of Lemons and Main

In the car-horn dawn the city bus
stops outside, blares

in loudspeak through the bifold
opening door the name

of this stop I already know.
We live curbside pushed up against

each day's watery swell
and ebb of commuters. Lately,

a Muslim woman in all-black garb,
head to toe so only her eyes show,

waits here mornings
dandling an exuberant child.

Frankie next door who works nights
says she must live in the rentals

near the Civil-War-era clay pit
which for decades was a landfill

and later a raised-up, gassy city park.
Nobody stays there long, he says.

We have stayed here a scholarly
long time, my teeth clenched

at passersby plucking our rose bush.
But the soil is not all sour.

LETTER FROM THE CORNER OF LEMONS AND MAIN

As I am writing this to you now,
our pre-school sons

are piling the floral couch cushions,
damming an imaginary river,

the younger one an elegant pink
flamingo stabbing

for shrimp in the New England fall,
amid the vanishing tannins

of leaf season. I don't know
if it matters at all where we stand.

Wish List in Middle Age

A bedroom for each child, a paid-for car,
tax holidays, maybe a few groupies or
the Prize Caravan arriving to film our bloom
of sudden wealth, less pushback and lip
from the pre-teen, small rocks at hand
for the drunk mockingbird, Tuesday after
Tuesday of fresh love-making, new vanities
and mirrors, perfect self-exams in salted, skin-
loosening baths, acceptance letters of various kinds,
new clothes to hide the wear of doing-it-ourselves.

My Resurrected Body

So what it took me longer than three
breaking dawns, returning
from the gym each morn overripe

in the nose of waking kids.
No one ever rubbed me
in fragrant oils. No sobbing

woman ever wrapped my ill
hamstring in her loving embrace
or an Ace bandage.

I was back before anyone missed me.
I never descended into hell,
but the floor these days

is a long way down, so how about
some applause for pulling myself
up from an early grave?

If you don't appreciate my
slimness, surely the Risen Lord
felt joy like mine when he came to,

noticed the extensors ripple
from the wrist as he strummed
the guitar to lead them in praise.

How can joy not lead to praise?
In the mirror of their singing
around the campfire, imagine

how his tanned skin shone
like a cosmos or a bright blue pill,
as he wiped the tears from their eyes.

Painstaker

To climb into the miniature car
I catch my nail on the tiny door,
close-stooped, surgical,
as if laying open an insect wing.

To stuff into the toy, I rear up
tall as a pole or roostered top
of a spire. I aim my toe like the tip
of an arrow at the street-level

small door. The surgeon scrubbing up
concedes my single-mindedness
(loved ones helpless watching
have called ahead).

To pierce the tiny door,
I align each vertebra expertly,
as if targeting the curve
warping free from the wand

of dollar-store bubbles.
If only I were an arrow skyward
I would leave childish things
surgically behind,

but I am no explosion
bought from *YHWH's Guns & Ammo*
of Aurora and Downer's Grove.
Such is the message each day

in the data. Practice your stoop,
it says. You are stuffing for the bird.
You must shrink yourself to a jot,
small as hum, serif

        of ink on a miniscule of snow.

Love Wins

I kill myself for you
daily and over the years,
leaping off

tall buildings
in a single bound, turning
lightning-struck bird,

or sucked out
the cabin door when I
imagine it opening

mid-flight. The key
is constructing
the scene ahead of time,

what they call
ideation or taking pains
or conscious hallucination,

followed by prim shock
at all it costs me and you
can't spare

one dime-sized tear?
We live trick
by trick, which is why

I am intimate
with the largest, most
merciful knife

LOVE WINS

in the drawer,
who pays no mind
to hesitation marks,

charges me the flat-rate,
opens up even when
the kitchen is closed.

It's the reason
I advertise sneaking off
to swim in shark-infested

waters. Because it plays
better on the big screen,
this lack of limb,

when I'm the torn lamb,
my red blood through the blue
like atomized perfume:

    I have it much worse than you.

Elegy for Deer-Man

As the deer panteth for flowing
streams, so pants my soul
and the dog in summer

who wears a fur coat
and pants. As the pant leg catches
in the bike chain, so the ants

that swarm the fallen
ice cream cone must make the ant-
version of lemonade

or else drown as the rising
seas eat up the concrete shoreline.
To say what I'm making

maybe it is a promise
to express those lemons,
those bright spots on the X-rays

whose acid brightness no one
will ever make sweet.
As you, like the deer-man,

take off your pants one leg
at a time, placing your glasses
on the night stand, breathing

becoming labored,
and rise to circle the fields leaping,
every muscle growing still.

Unbidden

Love keeps no record of wrongs.
They write themselves

like black mold on boards
from the torn-down shed, beaded

with pine sap where they sit
discarded in the clearing.

Daily through the tall grass we make
our visit, letting the dog

off leash to nose where she will.
Getting out like this is healthy,

pushing words out into the air
in front of us,

with each step letting the ragweed stir
and come what may.

Love keeps no record of wrongs.
They are written

like pins and screws in the fracture,
a weightless titanium.

Didn't you know
it is a miracle to be able to walk again.

Hope New Rising

I commute both ways into the sun
past the aggregate company where gravel
and dirt pile into a mound made by
trucks backing up in low gear unloading
then returning and backing the heap
up more, unloading week after week
until a road takes shape up the mound
made solid as rain-soak and packed
as a rammed-earth wall.
                                  Come April
I watch the mound begin to catch
with life as grass composes itself blade
by clump and watch what could be
a sapling sprung from shit of bird
shoot sideways before angling upward
driving roots toward old soil and O
I rejoice, my Lord, that all may rebuild,
come home, make for the heights, grow lush.

re Controversy

    For Larycia

I teach evangelical and ink
my name plainly, let it hang
there so I rise plane-like
all these pounds of me
bad joints and the strain
of flight muscles: *Hey,
check it out! Look at me!*
It's like magic I can soar
this high, though note
I didn't really say
magic only "magic"
in scare quotes (my fingers
are invisible here), so let
the record show. Besides
"It's" is deliberately vague
like a glued-on mustache
very macho kind of disco
sliding from the lip
as I sit here sweating
in the interrogation room.
Maybe I shouldn't admit
this to you or even think
of you as my neighbor
but the Lord is my
lightning rod, I shall fear
no media shit storm or
penny-sized hail
dimpling the car roof
and the June soybeans.
Benefit of the doubt is
a basic, civil right (notice I

RE CONTROVERSY

do not refer to doubt *per se*).
Words mean a lot
in this place, walk around
with their chests puffed out.
But let me just say, when
the pit bulls strain against
the leash I hold, I am
walking, too. Behind
them with a baggie for
cleaning up, I am walking, too.

Poem with Italicized Phrases from a Student's Water-Stained Mythology Class Notes, Found Perched on a Vanishing Bank of Snow

Her sadness without her daughter.
And the other half it is bright

and fresh, symbolizing her happiness.
She wasn't less now, even though she felt like it

when the reckless child tore away

in Emilio's car. I was walking along trying
to unwind a little when I found them, and *the theme*

of this myth is finders' keepers.
I picked up the piece of paper

thinking it was snow, pen marks
like the pollution of cinders in winter,

someone's Korean shopping list. But then
the words became my language. It was November.

Now I dream of lucky Emilio. *This myth relates to me*

mainly because I am Greek and, like your voice,
you can't throw that away. The Greekness of her

and her daughter, both happier
for the tragedy, the independence bouncing

in their steps as they walk, opposite, away.

III.

Sonnet

I walked the dog off the cliff
back onto solid ground, the sad-eyed
blue dog who once upon a time

all he did was eat. Somehow who did what
no longer matters. We both think so.
As if I would not step out of the boat

with you now onto the level black air.
As if your hang-dog words did not stir
in me the same grit and pebble

roiled by my own deafening sea.
If I grow more distant the nearer you get,
then it becomes your turn. Of this

I know. We are strangers strung together,
rods and bells on the wind chime, the damp,
full sound as it kicks about in the storm.

Isaiah in the Cancer Ward

    Pale on the gurney,
he struggled to push away

my solace, my hovering need
to grow fat on his pain, wheeled

with him into the sanctum
of iodine and cold hands. When I beg

that I might take his place,
go under, be carved,

    I am accused of interloping,
morbid curiosity, putting-them-on.

After his treatments, I watch him
next door, neighbor

head-shorn, low-slung
    in the heat-soaked yard,

under spade-shaped leaves
that drink from an invisible hand.

    How to convey that I, too,
was struck by that hand.

Down in the Head

I fall apart by steps,
by trinket or pill, by a wink
or a nod over the line

or out on air
like the cotton tuft
of a pocket turned out.

I know, sure, *poor me*,
never truly as I want to be,
i.e., not threadbare

but fresh-born, bubble
steady-centered. Thus much
I freely tell, which tale

now all may tell. Just know
that if you mock these words
I will put a pin

through your heart-stuffing.
You who grow slack
as a doll. You who lack

sinew. Who are you to say
anyway, Mr. Glass-house?
I've seen you pucker

for the lemon that comes
as it has and does and ever
must spray its fine mist.

DOWN IN THE HEAD

I am the chipped
plate no longer circle-
perfect. *As if chosen.*

So let hurt tooth and root.
Let hurt build and rot
and grow in store

until it stares me down.
Somebody hold me down.
I'm about to you know what.

You know you do.

Isaiah in Chicagoland

He will roll you up tightly like a ball
and throw you into a large country,
or drop-kick your ass the length
of a football field, or maybe smack
into a stone wall. Take that,
Big World! You better stay away
or else you'll end up splayed
on the ground open-mouthed, wind
knocked out, as the cheers go up
and the city beams, beckoning.

How hopeless the effort against the LORD!
How solid the city, its bricked-up peace!
How infinite the grass-fed beef!
The cloth diapers! The single-origin coffee!

We will drag the shop teacher
from his welder, wrench the boxer
from his jump rope, the professor
from her lecture on the waggle dance
of the honey bee. We will heat up
and raise hands to the tattooed church band.

Be warned, you rulers of the earth.

Shop-soiled, *adj.*

1. Exposed for sale in a shop on fire / a caterwaul blaze / cat-screaming flames; / thus exposed, made fallen / and subject to fire sale. Also, *fig*: the fallen hero / monikered / water-stained monarch / of city ash-pit.

2. "Soiled" is to be distinguished from "steeped in rich black soil fresh-turned" (*Obs.*, glacial, Wisconsin drift sheet) or (what you first thought) "the film of grease resulting from the practice of the automotive arts," the latter removed only at great effort using the grit of pumice stone soap.

3. Used explicitly of a man in certain straits: He walks with her youthful glow beside him, beside the visible fire of her bosom, beside the river, and beside (*lit.*) himself (disembodied, floating in the upper left hand corner of the frame, conscious of every jot and tittle she moves in him as she walks). He gets twisted up in himself because he is damaged goods, a husband once-removed, a one-time cheating tom. How to start again at the mid-point?

The Poet Abuzz after Chemo on a Whammo Steroid

    To the tune of Hendrix's "Voodoo Child"

Stir the sugar in your coffee with a tree branch
chop it down

with the edge of your puffed-up, neuropathic hand
into firewood, do a head stand

Crammed with inkhorn drugs you're gonna
saw up Cancer Mountain

with a rubber band, stomach the acne
and hair gone white

so you don't get canned, write all night
on this speedball
                      filling your glass with sand

Early Christian Advice Column

Do not leer or foul or filth.
Do not force air
across a bottle mouth

when you must do more.
Do not cool to the touch
or turn steam.

Do not play the diviner.
Do not skewer or schism or be
with others overly

harsh,
which leads to snare,
which saps the last cent.

Do not spoil the rod
by sparing my all.
Do not go or ungird.

(O, what I wouldn't
school myself to do
for You.)

Do not make or admit idols.
Do not idle or burn.
Do not turn.

New Life, Lake Scituate

Fall backward to disappear
into the water.
                       Ask the preacher
to let you stay down a while,

and when you rise up into the air your ears
and eyes turn on again so strongly

it seems you no longer need them.
                       But you do.

In the news this weekend a musician,
one mother, and three teenage boys canoeing

capsized or cramped up, the air
turning to lake silt and quarry-dark.

                 Newly taken by faith,
you still must flinch. Shun dark alleys. Test
your brakes.

              In some ways all is not forgiven.

Prayer

White kid from Kenya straps
a hammock between campus ash trees
planted when his missionary parents
were only a glimmer

in their own missionary parents'
full-to-bursting eyes of faith,
barely containing the urge to unloose
the sky. I imagine their want,

how they yearned to be His bride
full-stop and alert in the bush
awaiting the point of Jim Elliot's spear.
Now that their want is becoming his want,

I wonder about my own.
Who knows what I want is the One
who listens in on all sides.
The Lord is Who and always How,

so He is aware that here in this spot
is not where I planned to end up,
up-ended in myself, talking aloud
out of doors. Do You please

make sense of me. Make me
sensible and at peace with myself.
Teach me the calm of this odd-bird kid
who floats his nest between trees.

Elevation, St. Louis Arch

Eventually everyone's gone up inside,
claiming to feel it sway a little

like standing quickly after a few drinks,
when I wobble, off-center but still able

to walk smoothly over the floor of the bar
to where she sits talking with friends.

The elevator bubble rises lighter than air
up a silver groove

to surface immaterial, free from the taint
of the bars nearby,

from which I stumble and catch
its scaly night shine.

As I stand there bruised and alone,
a heart attack stops a casino boat winner.

For what reason would he not rise
from the rush of hands to his chest,

from the red lights and sirens,
    up through the needle's eye?

Elegy for a Poet Catching Stride

1.

My nethers swollen, sore, sketched
by the surgeon in pre-surgery on a piece
of scrap paper as he goes over

the *game plan* one more time,
which sketch I then quickly, nervously
tuck into your gorgeous debut

volume of poems, which poems
I brought with me not knowing
your words would end up

gently wrapping the deviant fruit
of my body the way newsprint
wrapped fish at that Irish restaurant

in Brookline. Would you spark
at the intimacy of the surgeon's
sketch, groan at my bad taste

in wanting to describe the proximity
of my nethers to the smooth cheek
of your author's photo? Our joking

has always proved deep waters.
Maybe what I'm really asking
is whether you live in your lines

the way I still meet you there.

2.

I should probably aim higher,
not merge your memory with my
experience of urological misfortune,

out of respect for the dead
and all that, quit trying to use
humor as a screen for tangled emotion.

Acting the wag is our thing, though.
Besides, in this account of pre-surgery
I am the one mock-worthy

in fuzzy socks, the biohazard
waiting to happen. Factually,
it's true your poems were

at my side when the handsome
surgeon arrived like a police
sketch artist, saying *here and here*

is what we'll do just so,
and the stitches will dissolve
the way everything dissolves just so,

so so long after you hobble
out of here leaning on your wife
as a crutch.

3.

If this is a game, nobody wins.
There is no way you can be beaten,
having already lost. My ill

is nothing like the news
of your cancer and the scarf-length
of colon they cut from you,

and then only months later the news
that the cells had snaked
from the colon into liver and lymph

and no more could be done,
no more but double-down
on our game of gentle insult,

ignore the gurgle of bile
exiting your fresh-cut *stoma*,
use the indecorous mock to somehow

cut through the brain fog
wrought by the pain meds, the days
you spent starving on waves

of Dilaudid until the brain
addled and you made no sense
so Elaine and David brought

the Lord's Table to your door
and we stood with you
the only way we knew how,

together tasting
the Lord who is broken
for all the ways we break down.

I Dream Your Face the Night You Move Away

Big blinding slates, star-like, empty, the blanks
in your sparse beard

are dazzling billboards that each night singe the grass
bent toward them. No word plays,

no enticements to buy, no cows
swishing their tails alongside the highway

in the dark. Where is this I've followed you?
Not billboards   screens at an outdoor

multiplex theater we come to
for your last night in town. You, the attraction.

The scent of popcorn turns our sadness
to anticipation, but the glow

of the blank screens shows you've disengaged.
         At some point I want to see the celluloid

redden, brief flood of roses on the wallpaper, pools of blush

at your own good fortune, able to leave us
so far away. Nothing   then the bulb

burns out over the kitchen table
and you slip off. As we wait, your light forces in

             blinding for an instant,
as you back out of the driveway, carried away.

Winter Monarchs, *Michoacán*

   i.m. Casey Luebbert (1971–1992)

Some fall to earth
    before the mountain looms,

but millions mate and ornament the trees
once there, trunk and leaf

under a surge of orange. The land
is a weight in the blood so strong

   that most will let down
their wings, wings leaden

as his arms in the night water, lost
for days, then dredged,

wrestled to shore in a fishing net.
Better to remember him

home, cocksure and prized,
                          hazard for the crow.

Killdeer

Some birds limp, drag one wing, or cry
to lure danger from their young. When the bird in me
feigned it was broken, I saw myself whole, strong-limbed, yet

to age. Through barn shadow and stand
of pine, I ran from the foreclosed-on farm, schoolboy
striking at prairie sedge and compass plants,

clouds of long-tongued bees. Back
at the feed lot, animals at war
for the blessing of my red-stung, outstretched arms.

Self-Portrait as Motel Night Clerk

1.

Jerry stands at the desk in bitch-face,
hand on hip, joking that our Hindu boss
would step over a dollar

to save a dime. He likes to rant, likes
that I will listen, calls me *sweetheart*,
but the long hours are pulling

at his face after selling rooms
all day. Besides, it's graveyard-time
and I need to lock myself inside, verify

the small window will slide open
for the a.m. rush of hard-up guests.
Jerry warns me about Pimp Charming,

young Silver-Tongue, who's been around
with his girl. Do not rent him rooms.
I'm eager to get to work on my list of late-

night loves. The menu tonight: a delicious
fiction prompt, a passage from John's
Gospel, and maybe in the wee hours

an action flick from off the rental shelf.
You shouldn't plan too much. Leave
to chance what bubbles up.

2.

After Jerry leaves, it's just me for a while
until the bars close and she calls me,
because she knows no matter

what she's done I will never hang up.
The fraternity boy she took home,
whom she let do an unspeakable act,

has left. *Why am I like this*, she says.
Then tenderly, *Read to me from the Bible.*
Open it anywhere you want.

When I grow tired from reciting
the Word, she wants to tell me
how it felt, the encounter like

she wasn't there or it wasn't even her.
And then she reminds me how
God spoke to her once, made

it clear that she and I were designed
for each other. He knit us together
in the womb, in the stars,

even before our mothers conceived us.
So I say, having no other words,
that she is wonderfully, fearfully made.

3.

Pimp Charming won't harm me, says
he'll cut me in, let me sample the goods.
I hear all manner of truth on this job.

One night, a heavy-set woman taps on
the window holding her stomach,
wanting a bed to lie down in after

the surgery must not have gone right
because it feels like the staples
are coming loose and *Oh God,*

she says, *my guts are going to spill!*
Or the delicate teen from the tour bus
of Mormon kids who sneaks back

to the lobby to break her heart
to me, expose her ticking faith
the way I spoke God's love

to Mexican street kids or beach drunks
in Daytona on spring break.
She leaves me her Book of Mormon

with a prayer that one day I'll find
the truth. As if holding up a mirror
to my own pleading face.

4.

I believe every one of them,
just as I believe the woman
who races from country town

to the university hospital.
Her tap-tap at the window. Will I
unlock the door because she

won't make it another mile. *I don't want
an ambulance*, she says, when I offer.
After letting her in, I bring a cup

of water, sit down beside her
as the interstate rushes by outside.
The country doctor said take

to the road, get to the big hospital,
so here she is with only
a few hours left to live. Her lids

are heavy, speech not quite right,
until she panics mid-
sentence, shoves back

from the table. *I'm contagious,*
she says, *I'm contagious and you're
so kind*, tripping on her way to

the door, fumbling with the lock into
the parking lot as I am
running after her *What is it?*

What do you have? She waves me off
with pepper spray, warning
not a step closer or she'll hurt me.

It's bad, she says. *You don't want this*,
slipping into her car
and I watch her drive off.

5.

Years later I decide to push back.
Dig out your ears, the preacher says.
So I keep my own cards close, step on

a few toes, look to add more notes to my song.

Two Decades Gone, *Barra de Navidad*

Although the waters pull you down no more,
perhaps now the bayside town

has search and rescue,
workers skilled in spotting you,

able to hook and bear you
on glistening paramedic boats to shore.

Imagine that homecoming, that looming world.

Isaiah on the Promise of International Space Projects

It will take much longer

than sixteen countries working metal plates
in the heat of great fires, more than lifetimes
or the moneys of diverse currencies or many

rivers muscling into one faster, stronger flume,
to project the heart so large

and weightless, a floating Babel

of bared emotions, into the black sky.
It will take more than years
to project the heart so large, the weaving

of arms lifted up in the music of intense praise
away from the earth, braid after

braid into one glowing rope spiraling
beyond all that weighs, constricts

and blankets.
At which point will begin the age of invisible buoys

and giant stars, the era of light.

Made in the USA
Columbia, SC
05 January 2019